Alien Adventures

Cyberbee
Break Out

Mike Tucker • Jonatronix

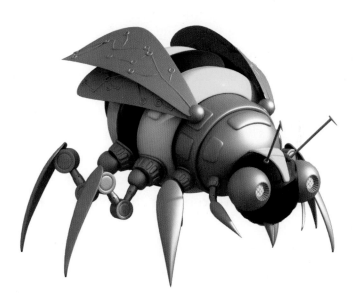

OXFORD

UNIVERSITY PRESS

Max's mission log

We are travelling through space on board the micro-ship Excelsa with our new friend, Eight.

We are trying to get home. Our only chance is to get to the Waythroo Wormhole – a space tunnel that should lead us back to our own galaxy. We don't have long. The wormhole is due to collapse very soon. If we don't get there in time, we'll be trapped in the Delta-Zimmer Galaxy forever!

To make matters worse, a space villain called Badlaw is following us in his Destroyer ship. Badlaw and his army of robotic Krools want to take over Earth. We can't let that happen!

Our new mission is simple: to shake off Badlaw and get to the Waythroo Wormhole before it collapses. I just wish it was as easy as it sounds.

Time until wormhole collapses: 2 days, 2 hours and 10 minutes

In our last adventure ...

Badlaw offered a reward for capturing the Excelsa and a greedy pirate, Captain Greenbeak, couldn't resist the prize. He hooked our ship using an energy line!

Cat came up with a plan to distract the pirates so they wouldn't hand us over to Badlaw – she pretended to show the captain the way to a planet made of solid gold.

Captain Greenbeak wasn't fooled for long. He made Cat walk the plank! But, in the nick of time, Eight freed the Excelsa and we shot to Cat's rescue.

Chapter 1 – Distress signal

The Excelsa zoomed through the silence of space. There was no time to lose. They only had two days, two hours and ten minutes left before the Waythroo Wormhole was due to collapse!

While Tiger steered the ship, the rest of the crew were gathered around Cat's navigation console, arguing. Space might be silent, but the Excelsa wasn't!

"This is the quickest route," said Cat firmly.

"If we go that way it will take us into the radiation wasteland," argued Eight. "It's too dangerous. This route is safer." She traced a line on the screen with a mechanical finger.

"We're running out of time," Cat pointed out. "We have to go through the wasteland, no matter how dangerous it is."

Tiger rolled his eyes. He was about to butt in when a siren echoed around the bridge.

"It's an Intergalactic Distress Signal," said Eight. Ant dashed back to his desk and studied the control panel. "It's coming from a planet nearby."

"We should go and investigate," said Tiger, gripping the steering orbs, ready to change course.

"Hold on a minute, Tiger," said Ant. "How do we know this isn't one of Badlaw's traps?"

They all looked at Max. As the captain, it was his decision.

Max's mind spun as he weighed up the options. "What if someone needs our help? We can't just leave them," he said finally.

Ant pushed the controls and a fact file flashed on to his screen. "The planet is called Florian," he read. "It's a jungle planet and, according to this, there shouldn't be any machines or technology of any sort down there."

"Well, it looks like there's something down there *now*," said Max. "Take us down, Tiger."

Planet Florian

Planet Florian is on the outskirts of the Delta-Zimmer Galaxy. It is covered in a colourful jungle and is rich in plant and animal life. It has been described as an 'unspoiled paradise' as there is no technology of any sort on the planet.

Known life forms

▶ Too many species to mention

Surface conditions

▶ Humid and tropical

▶ Dense jungle

jungle ●●○○○○○○○○○

sea ●●○○○○○○○○○

tropical, hazy atmosphere ●●○○○○○○○

Chapter 2 – Hestan

The engines roared as the Excelsa swooped down towards Florian. Just minutes later the micro-ship was settling on to the ground in a leafy clearing.

Cautiously the micro-friends made their way down the holo-ramp. When they were clear of the ship, they each pressed their buttons and grew to normal size, staring in wonder at their surroundings. It was a jungle but unlike any jungle on Earth.

Trees reaching hundreds of feet into the air surrounded them. Strange football-sized orange and purple fruit hung from huge branches, and yellow-leaved bushes covered the ground. Everything looked lush and unspoiled.

"This place is amazing," said Tiger, looking around at the alien plants.

Eight pushed a button on her chest and turned on the ship's cloaking device. "Just in case," she said, as their ship disappeared.

"Which direction is the distress signal coming from?" asked Cat, eager to get going.

"This way," said Eight, setting off through the trees.

Before long they came across a steep slope in the forest floor. Broken branches lay everywhere. Looking down, the friends could see a bulky, white spaceship at the bottom of a crater. There was a huge rip in its metal skin.

"Looks like it was quite a crash," said Tiger, eyes widening. "I hope the crew got out OK."

"Let's take a look," said Max.

The friends scrambled down the slope towards the spaceship.

As they got closer Max called out, "Hello ... Is anybody in there?"

Inside, the spaceship was a mess. Broken control panels and loose wires lay everywhere. Slumped in the pilot's chair was a motionless figure.

The friends clustered around the pilot.

"It's a robot!" Tiger said, spinning the chair around. "I don't think he has any power though."

"Can you help him, Eight?" asked Cat.

"I'll try." Eight hovered forward. A thin metal rod extended from one of her fingers and slotted into a socket in the side of the motionless robot's head.

There was a sudden buzz of power. The robot's metal eyelids slowly started to open, and a soft blue light began to glow on its chest.

"It worked!" cried Ant.

"Oh, my," said a deep, mechanical voice. "I do believe we're going to crash! Help!"

"It's a bit late to be asking for help," said Tiger. "You've already crashed!"

"It's OK," Max said, reassuringly. "You're safe now. We got your distress signal."

The robot turned to look at him. "Oh, thank you. Thank you so much."

"I'm Max. This is Cat, Ant and Tiger. And that's Eight."

The robot rose from his seat and looked at each of them in turn.

"Delighted to meet you. My name is Hestan. I'm a cargo pilot."

"What happened to you?" asked Cat.

"I'm not sure," explained Hestan. "One minute, I was flying along on course for my next delivery, when suddenly the ship went spinning out of control. There must have been some sort of system malfunction."

"I'll run a check of all the systems," said Eight. "I'm sure we'll be able to help."

"Um, there is actually another small problem," said Hestan. "Several hundred small problems in fact."

Chapter 3 – The small problem

"The ship crashed into a tree and that's as much as I can remember," explained Hestan. "I must have switched off automatically. It looks like my cargo have escaped though." He pointed to the hole in the side of his ship.

"Escaped?" Ant's eyes opened wide. "What sort of cargo was it?"

"A swarm of cyberbees," Hestan said, with a mechanical groan.

The friends looked at each other, confused.

"What are cyberbees?" asked Max.

"They are tiny robots," said Eight. "They work as a team – a swarm – and they can be programmed to perform dozens of different tasks."

"Unfortunately the swarm I was carrying hasn't been programmed yet," said Hestan worriedly.

"Left by themselves they'll operate at the most basic level," Eight said.

"That's right," continued Hestan. "They will build a nest and the queen will start programming the workers herself. Then they will just do whatever comes into their little robotic brains – whether it's helpful or not!"

"They could cause chaos on an unspoiled planet like this," added Eight.

"Well, let's try and capture them then," said Tiger.

"Hold on," said Cat. "Someone has to stay and help Eight and Hestan repair the ship."

"Ant knows the most about real insects," pointed out Max. "If anyone can find the cyberbees, it's him."

Cat nodded. "You go with him, Max. Tiger and I will stay here."

Cat saw Tiger's disappointment. "We need you here, Tiger. You're the best at fixing things."

Tiger was desperate to look round the jungle, but he knew that Cat was right.

Waving goodbye to their friends, Max and Ant headed off into the jungle.

Chapter 4 – Tracking the swarm

"We need to look for the cyberbees' nest," said Ant. "If we find the nest, we'll find the queen."

The boys set off at a brisk pace and, before long, they had left Hestan's ship far behind.

The air around them was filled with the sound of the clicks and hums from unfamiliar insects and the cries of alien birds.

Then they heard a different sound – a familiar sound. *NURP!* The boys exchanged a glance.

"Is that what I think it is?" asked Max.

"It's coming from this direction," said Ant, pushing through a thick tangle of undergrowth.

Max followed close behind. He gave a gasp of surprise at the sight that greeted them. "It's a herd of nurps!"

The friends had met the large, cow-like creatures on a previous adventure.

Suddenly the herd became agitated. They started to flick their heads around and snort loudly.

"Hey! What's wrong with them?" Ant asked.

The nurps were swatting at the air with their trunks. As Max and Ant crept closer to the herd, they became aware of a harsh buzzing sound.

A hazy cloud surrounded the nurps. Max and Ant could see hundreds of small metal objects swirling above them.

"It must be the cyberbee swarm!" cried Ant.

They watched as the swarm circled the herd like a cloud of glitter hovering in mid-air. The jungle was filled with the sound of annoyed 'nurping'.

Then, suddenly, the herd turned and started to gallop towards Max and Ant.

"Nurp stampede!" shouted Max.

"Quick, Max. Shrink!" yelled Ant.

The two friends shrank to micro-size just as the nurps reached them. They sheltered behind a rock as the herd thundered past.

After a few moments the micro-friends peered out from their hiding place. The nurps had gone. So had the swarm of cyberbees.

"Quick!" cried Max. "Before we lose the swarm! Let's fly!"

The friends released their holo-wings and followed the swarm to a huge tree.

"They've gone up there," said Ant, zooming up. The top of the trunk was punctured with lots of little holes. "This must be the cyberbees' nest," he whispered. "The queen will be in there for sure."

Chapter 5 – Sabotage!

Back at the crashed ship, Tiger, Eight and Hestan had just finished repairing the hole in the side of the ship. Next they had to replace some damaged components. Cat was reading out instructions to them. It all seemed very complicated.

"I wonder how Max and Ant are getting on," she muttered.

Tiger frowned at her. "If you are getting bored then you could always come and help."

"What, when you're doing such a great job?" said Cat, grinning.

"Actually, there is something that you can both help with," interrupted Eight. She hovered across to the control desk. "I still haven't found the system fault that caused the crash. I need you to shrink and check the main console for me."

Cat and Tiger shrank to micro-size. Picking them up, Hestan carefully placed them on the control console.

"You need to get to the main steering circuits," he said. "If they're damaged, they will be all burnt and blackened."

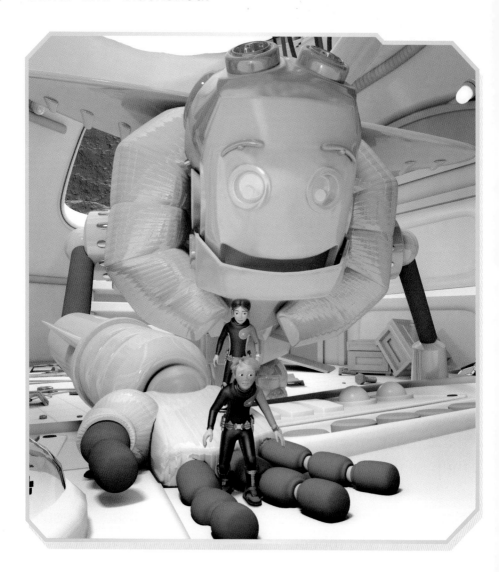

Cat and Tiger jumped down inside the control panel. Thick wires were hanging down like creepers around them. It was like being in a metal version of the jungle outside.

"The steering circuits are right at the bottom of the control panel," said Hestan, peering in through the gap in the console.

The micro-friends tiptoed carefully across the circuit boards. Tiger took the lead, using the torch on his watch to light the way.

Before long, they were deep inside the workings of the spaceship.

"Follow the blue wires," shouted Hestan from above.

They did as instructed and soon came to the end of the blue wires. The wires weren't burnt or blackened at all, but something was definitely wrong.

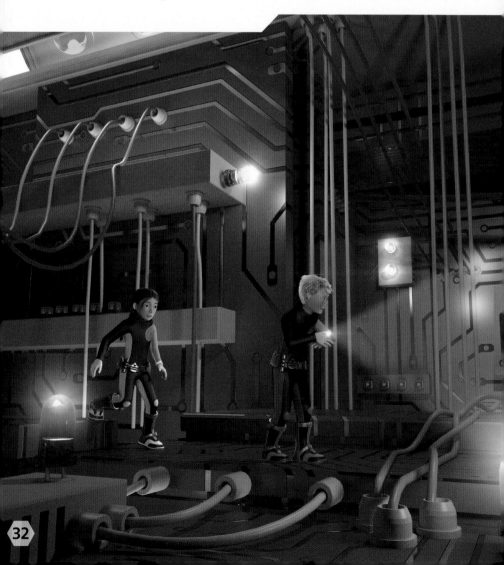

Cat and Tiger hurried forward to take a closer look.

Tiger directed his torch at the circuits. Cat knelt and looked at the wires hanging limply down from their ports.

"Tiger, these wires look like they've been cut," said Cat. "Someone, or something, has done this deliberately."

"That means there wasn't a system failure at all," said Tiger. "It was sabotage!"

Chapter 6 – Into the nest

Max and Ant stared into a deep hole in the tree trunk.

"What are we going to do when we find the queen?" asked Ant.

"I'll make contact with Eight and see what she suggests," said Max.

A hologram of Eight soon formed from Max's watch. Max repeated Ant's question.

"Once you've found the queen, Hestan will send a signal via your watches that will stop her in her tracks. We can give you further instructions then," Eight explained.

It was dark inside the hole and the boys could hear the beating of metallic wings. With a nervous glance at each other, the two friends clambered inside.

It took a moment for their eyes to get accustomed to the gloom. Then the two of them set off into the nest.

Suddenly something scuttled out in front of them.

The micro-friends pressed themselves against the wall. It was a cyberbee. It had six metal legs and a yellow and black striped body. Two sharp pincers jutted out from underneath its head and at the tip of its tail there was the sting, gleaming like a curved sword.

"Just keep still," whispered Ant. "If it's anything like bees on Earth, it won't bother us."

The cyberbee moved towards them.

"Oh, no!" said Max. "It heard you!"

The cyberbee loomed over the micro-friends, examining them with its camera-like eyes. They could hear motors whirring as its robot brain tried to work out what it was seeing.

Then it gave an angry buzz. It jerked its head and moved forwards again, forcing the boys deeper into the nest.

"We'd better go where it wants us to," whispered Ant.

They made their way along the tunnel and soon they emerged into a large chamber. The boys gasped. In the centre was a robot much larger than the others. The smaller bees were crowded round it. Max and Ant had found the queen.

All the cyberbees suddenly turned to look at the intruders. The nest began to buzz with the noise of hundreds of metallic wings as the bees advanced towards them.

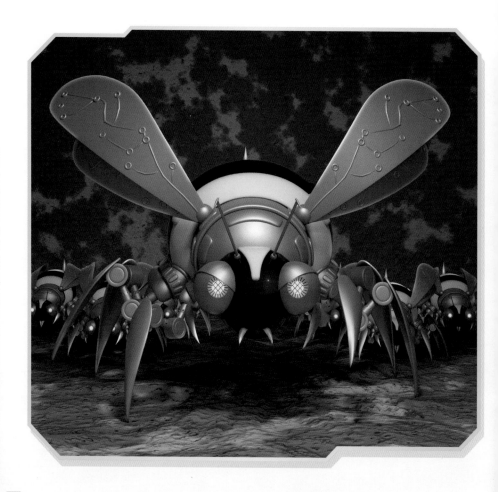

Chapter 7 – Circuit breakers

"Max!" shouted Ant. "Call Eight! Quickly! Get Hestan to send the signal!"

Max fumbled with the communicator button on his watch. "Eight! Help! We've found the queen, but I think we've upset her."

Just then, Ant stumbled backwards and crashed into the bee that had led them to the chamber. It gave an angry buzz and raised its sting.

Suddenly the hologram of Eight appeared on Max's watch and an electronic noise blared around the nest. All the cyberbees froze.

Hestan's deep voice came over the communicator. "You'll need to open up the inspection panel on the queen's back. Follow my instructions."

The two boys made their way through the ranks of motionless cyberbees to the queen. Max clambered up on to her metallic back and Ant followed.

There was a small, square panel just behind the queen's head – the inspection panel. Carefully Max prised it open. A tangle of electronic circuitry spilled out.

Following Hestan's step-by-step instructions, Max and Ant adjusted the controls so that the queen would listen to Ant's voice and follow his orders.

"The queen will now follow any commands that you give, Ant," said Hestan. "Get the swarm back to the ship."

Max and Ant activated their wings. "Queen of the cyberbees," shouted Ant, "I order you to follow me!"

With a whirr, the wings of the queen started to beat. The other bees copied. Max and Ant zoomed off down the passageway ... and the cyberbees followed.

Ant whooped with delight as they flew high over the Florian jungle, the swarm following obediently behind them.

Chapter 8 – Stowaway

"It's Max and Ant!" shouted Tiger, pointing to a screen. "Look! They're leading the swarm."

Quickly Hestan opened the door of the cargo hold and the swarm flew in. "I must go and count them!" said Hestan. "I have to make sure all my cargo has been returned safely."

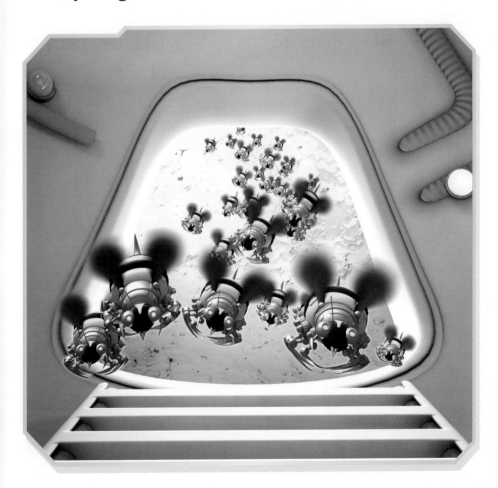

Hestan vanished into the cargo hold. Cat and Tiger could hear him counting.

"Five, ten, fifteen, twenty ... Now stay still, you're making it difficult! Oh, I'll have to start again. Five, ten ..."

After a few minutes, Hestan reappeared in the doorway. "Oh dear!" he said. "There still seems to be a problem."

"What's wrong?" asked Cat. "Are we missing some bees?"

"No!" cried Hestan. "We've got one too many!"

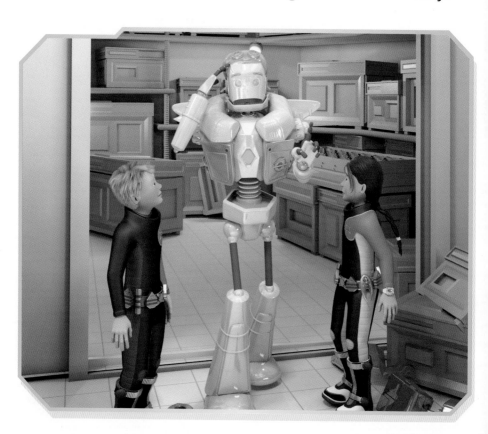

The children and Eight crowded into the cargo hold. Each of the cyberbees had settled into a compartment in a large honeycomb-shaped crate. One bee was just hovering aimlessly. There was no space left for it to go.

Eight scooped up the bee carefully. "This one is different from the others," she said, examining it closely.

She turned it over. "I thought so. Look. It's Badlaw's symbol."

"This is no cyberbee! It is a Kroolbee. This has been sent by Badlaw!" Eight continued. "It's got some sort of radio transmitter on it!"

"That makes sense," said Tiger angrily. "When Cat and I went to look at the steering circuits, we found wires had been cut deliberately. There was no system failure. It must have been this Kroolbee all along."

"Badlaw must have guessed that we'd pick up the distress signal and come to help," said Ant thoughtfully. "I bet he planned for this bee to sneak aboard the Excelsa so he could track us to Earth."

"We should dismantle it," said Tiger, reaching out for the bee.

"I think I've got a better idea," said Hestan, starting to reprogramme the bee. "If Badlaw wants to follow this bee, he can follow it ... into the radiation wasteland!"

The four children watched as Hestan's ship vanished into the sky. He would release the Kroolbee as soon as he was clear of the planet.

"Come on, we had better get going too!" said Max. "Hestan's trick may put Badlaw on the wrong scent but we still need to make up for lost time."

"We've only got one day left to get to the wormhole now!" said Cat.

Find out what happens next in
Operation Holotanium.